50 Essential Business Advice Tips To Prevent Your Business From Failing

I0463238

By Paul Green, FInstIB
www.paulgreen.biz

First published in Great Britain in 2011
by paulgreen.biz

Copyright © 2011 Paul Green – www.paulgreen.biz

ISBN 978-1-4565463-1-1

Disclaimer – no responsibility can be accepted for any actions that you take as a result of the contents provided in this guide. There is no guarantee that implementing any of these tips will definitely prevent your business from failing. They are presented as a guide based on the experience of the author working with many different types of business and are provided as a choice for you to consider if they will make an impact on your business. If in any doubt, please seek the assistance of a qualified professional.

Contents

Introduction

No one wants to fail in business; however, statistics show that 1 in 3 businesses fail in the first year of trading and a further 50% of the remainder don't progress after the third year.

Whatever stage your business is at, this guide aims to give you the essential elements that you should have in place to prevent your business from failing.

Split into sections, this guide covers all 'pillars' of business: Strategy, Finance, Sales, Marketing, Operations, Resources & Personal.

If you find this guide is useful to you, your feedback and comments are very much welcomed and appreciated - please email tips@paulgreen.biz with your thoughts.

I look forward to hearing from you.

Here's to the success of your business.

Best regards,

Paul

Strategy

☐ **Vision** - what was your dream when you started your business? Is it still relevant today and are you achieving it?

Having something to ultimately aim for is what motivates and gets you out of bed in the morning. If you have lost your way with this vision, take a moment (or longer) to reconnect with what the reason was that you disconnected with the corporate rodent race and decided to go it alone.

Write your vision down and have it be a foundation for rekindling your business and the basis of taking action on the tips in this guide.

☐ **Planning** - are you planning to fail by failing to plan? If you don't know where you are heading, how will you know when you get there?

A 'working' business plan is essential to capture the objectives for the business; it should be a dynamic document that is regularly reviewed and adapted as the business grows, with specific, measurable targets and associated actions of who is doing what by when.

This overall plan should be communicated to staff throughout the business and each department should have their own plan in line with the overall plan.

(A free business plan template can be downloaded at www.paulgreen.biz/downloads.htm)

☐ **Exit** - when you started the business did you have an idea of what you wanted to achieve and what the exit strategy might be?

Most people go into business to make money and secure their future - the sale of a profitable business could form the basis of your financial independence. If you know what your expectations are and the timescales, you can manage and plan your business accordingly to maximise the return you get when you come to sell the business.

This is where it is important to have a mid-term (3 years) and long-term (5 years) business plan to help manage your business to the point where you exit.

To help you with your business planning, Business Plan Pro is award winning software with over 500 business plan templates to assist you in writing a comprehensive business plan: http://tinyurl.com/bplanpro

Finance

☐ **Cashflow** - cash is king for any business and is the main cause of business failure. Knowing where your cash is, what is coming in, what is going out and how much you have is crucial. Ensure that you know how money moves around within your company.

(A free cashflow template can be downloaded at www.paulgreen.biz/downloads.htm)

☐ **Credit Control** - to support your cashflow, chase invoices before they are due i.e. 7 days before; make sure there are no issues that could cause a delay in settling the invoice and that you are on the payment run. If there are problems, they can be resolved in advance so there is no delay in payment being made to you; or, if the client has a problem paying, you can come to a suitable agreement. With regard to creditors, don't pay too early and negotiate the best terms you can and, if you are having problems paying, communicate with your supplier and see if you can arrange a payment plan to help your cashflow.

☐ **Management Accounts** - often bookkeepers and accountants provide figures that look backwards not forwards and maybe are up to 3 months out of date. Make sure that whoever is producing the finances for you, that they are preparing a cashflow forecast looking at the months ahead and that the key parameters for your business are being reported, so that you know at least monthly (if not weekly) exactly where you stand.

☐ **Break Even Point** - this is the minimum level of sales that you need to make to cover all your business costs and start to get into a profitable situation. Assuming you know your fixed costs (e.g. salaries, rent, rates - often referred to as overheads) and variable costs (these relate to the cost of production and vary with quantity e.g. raw materials) within the business, the simplest way to work this out is as follows:

Calculate Gross Profit (GP) = Total Sales - Variable Costs

Calculate your GP percentage = GP ÷ Total Sales

Break Even Point = Fixed Costs ÷ GP Percentage

The graph below illustrates an alternative way of looking at the break even point:

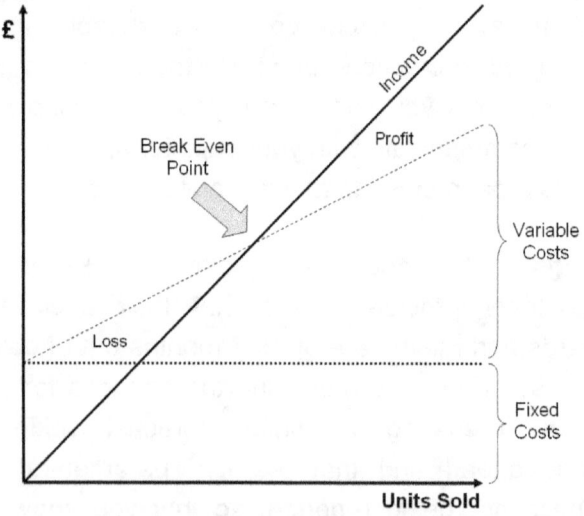

(To calculate your break even point, please try the free online calculator: www.paulgreen.biz/break_even.htm)

☐ **Cost Reduction** - do you have a handle on the costs in your business particularly for the supply of goods and services? It is worth reviewing at least annually to see where savings can be made or test the market regularly to assess if your suppliers are competitive in the current economic climate.

☐ **Grants** - make sure you are aware of any grants that may be available to your business. You maybe in a particular geographic region where funds are available, or have a specific niche (e.g. waste management, environmental services) where there may be particular specialist grants for your business.

There are also streams of funding for research and development, overseas trade, leadership development and you may even be eligible for EU grants. A useful site to search for grants is www.grantfinder.co.uk.

☐ **Funding** - are you aware of the various options available to fund your business? An overdraft or loan may not be the most cost effective way and there are a number of other ways of raising capital and improving cashflow for your business: factoring, leasing, asset finance, trade finance, payroll funding, pension funds, business angels and venture capitalists. If you are successful in raising funds for your business, invest it wisely and effectively so that it makes a difference to your business stability and growth.

(A useful article covering all the different types of funding that are available can be found here: http://tinyurl.com/types-funding)

- ☐ **Banks** - are you working with the right bank, one who understands your business and its needs? Maintain communication with your 'bank manager', keep them up to date on what is happening in the business; even if your situation is precarious - the bank will find out eventually. Keeping them 'on side' can benefit you if you have difficult decisions to make that may need your bank's support.

- ☐ **Profit versus Turnover** - there is a saying *"turnover is vanity, profit is sanity"*. What is the point of having millions of pounds of sales revenue but only pounds of profit? Know where and what your costs are to get your product and service to market and if you are actually making any money on the sales that you are making (see Break Even Point above). Don't wait for your annual accounts to appear a few months after the year end only to find out you have made a loss!

- ☐ **Invoicing** - consider increasing the frequency that your invoices are sent out - why wait until the end of the month? This means you can chase invoices earlier and just before they are due to ensure timely payment and improve your cashflow. This will depend on the terms and conditions and arrangement that you have with your clients - these can be changed if you think that 'instant invoicing' will benefit your business.

- ☐ **Capitalization** - having enough funds to run the business is key to being successful. If you are starting a business and you have no sales for 3 months, will you still be able to fund your marketing activity and other costs in the business?

Sales

☐ **Pricing** - don't be the cheapest in the market for what you do. Understand value versus price and what your value proposition is relative to your competitors. Be wary of discounting and consider putting your prices up - do you really know what your customer or prospect is prepared to pay for what you offer?

For example, if your margin is 40% and you reduce price by 10%, you need sales volume to increase by 33% to maintain the same profit. Likewise, a 10% increase in price could sustain a 20% reduction in sales volume without loss of profit (see graph below for other percentages):

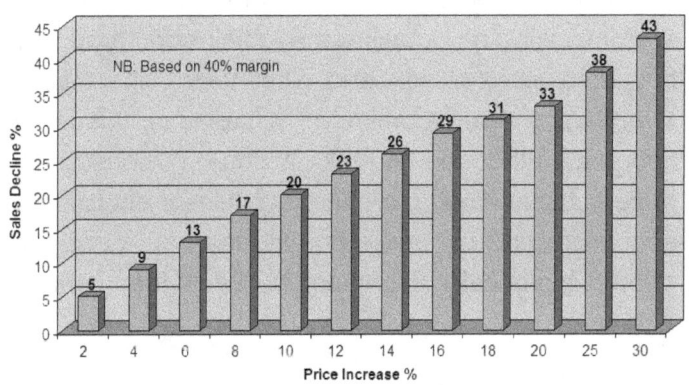

Therefore increasing your prices may not be so scary. The important thing here is to test your market before making a sweeping decision.

(For more information on price discounting - see http://tinyurl.com/price-discount; for price increasing - see http://tinyurl.com/price-increasing)

- [ ] **Up Selling** - the most common form of up selling is "*Do you want fries with that?*" – What is your version of this? If you have just made a sale or about to, what extras can you add while the customer is in a 'buying' mood?

- [ ] **Cross Selling** - similar to up selling but undertaken after any sale has been made by going back to the customer offering them something else that may be relevant to what they originally purchased or even a different product or service that you believe would be of interest. A good example of this is Amazon, who will offer customers other goods that relate to what they have just purchased or that were brought by other people buying the same thing.

- [ ] **Customers** - know your customer and know what they want. When was the last time you surveyed your customers to find out what they think about you, why they buy from you (or not) and what their expectations are? Even if you receive moans or complaints, this is valuable information that you can take action on to ensure that you have satisfied customers in the future. It could be a good source for product development ideas, as what you have offered historically might not be what the market wants today.

- [ ] **Customer Relationship Management** - it is important to maintain a relationship with customers and stay in communication and contact (not just via a monthly invoice!); possibly through newsletters, email bulletins, visits, open days, etc. If you're not doing it, your competition could be. It also keeps your brand in their mind on a regular basis.

☐ **Sales Pipeline** - have a system that manages where your potential customer is in the buying cycle so that you can interact with them accordingly from target, through to prospect, ready to make the decision to buy, the close and then after sales.

Measure conversion rates at each stage so that you can see if there are any weak links in the chain (often the closing part) and help you with making your marketing more effective.

The stages of a typical sales pipeline/funnel are illustrated in the diagram below:

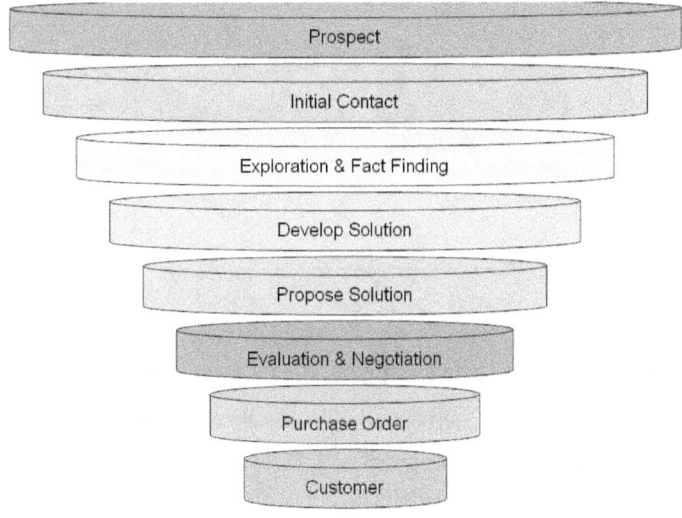

☐ **Sales People** - a heavy cost and burden for any business and the pressure is on for them to perform and bring in revenue; both for the employer and the sales person. Part of a recent survey indicated that less than a third (31%) of salespeople reviewed demonstrated proficiency in all eight core selling skills; therefore choosing the right person for your organisation is a 'minefield' and the cost to the business of employing the wrong candidate is substantial.

You may be interested to know where a poor sales person spends his time:

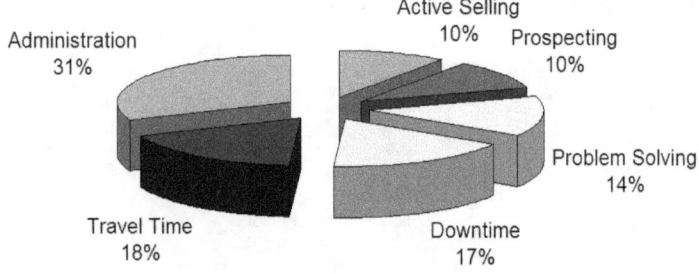

(To find out the percentages for a successful sales person -
www.paulgreen.biz/sales.htm)

The effective assessment of a sales person's ability is crucial before engaging such an expensive resource - there are tools available to help with this process - e.g. www.salesassessment.com - and there are options to outsource the sales process entirely to independent professionals who are primarily paid on results.

☐ **Joint Ventures/Strategic Alliances** - if you have a strong client base but have exhausted what you sell to them i.e. what you offer may only be a one off purchase - a will for example; or you don't have a suitable 'up sell' or 'cross sell' offering, it is worth considering a partnership with a non-conflicting organisation that would be interested in your clients' demography.

As you have the trust of someone who has brought from you in the past, there is a higher possibility that they will buy from you again even if the product/service is through a joint venture/strategic alliance with another company.

Using the 'will example' - a health care company maybe interested in a customer base that has recently purchased a will. The key here is to choose a reputable company so that it does not damage your reputation with your client base. There is also a good chance of it being a two way relationship such that your offering could be presented to their customers.

Marketing

☐ **Website** - a high percentage of SMEs do not have a website or have a very poor representation on line. The first thing a prospect is likely to do when looking to make a purchase is to 'Google' it or even if they have found your company in a directory, through an advert or via a leaflet through the door, it is likely they will try to find your website to 'check you out'.

A basic, professional internet presence does not have to be expensive and even a single page with some basic details about your company will suffice to start with. See: www.1and1.co.uk/?k_id=3945421

☐ **Email Address** - do you think a Yahoo, Hotmail, GMail, AOL or similar email addresses for your business conveys how you want your market to perceive you? As with the website, it is not costly to set up a 'co.uk' domain that reflects your business name and has associated email addresses with it, helping heighten the perception of your company. Take a look here for some available options: www.1and1.co.uk/?k_id=3945421

☐ **USP** - what is your Unique Selling Proposition? What is it that distinguishes you from your competitors and why would I consider buying from you as opposed to them? Being able to identify your competitive advantage(s) forms the foundation of your marketing message to your prospects.

☐ **Identify Your Market** - this may not be as obvious as it seems. Often companies try to be all things to all people, making it particularly hard to focus any marketing activity e.g. your message to a corporate would be different to that to an SME or to an individual consumer - whilst the product or service may be the same, the positioning will vary depending on who you are trying to reach.

If it is a 'cloud computing' service that you are selling, the benefits to an individual versus a company with 50 staff are entirely different. So, identify who an ideal client would be - who are your best (most profitable) clients now?

The premise for your 'perfect' customer could be based on geography, turnover, number of staff, role within a company, age, sex, industry sector or more than likely a combination of these and other contributory factors depending on the type of business you run.

Another point to consider is how many new customers do you want (can you handle) over the next 12 months? Let's say 10 for argument's sake - so if you could find 10 perfect customers over the next 12 months, would it be easier to find them from 1000 targeted prospects versus however big the market is you are trying to address right now?

The more specific (niche) you can be, the easier the targets are to identify and subsequently convert to clients.

☐ **Channels To Market** - as there is no definitive answer as to the best channel to market for your business, the recommendation is to have numerous, mixed and varied ways of accessing your potential clients with the proviso that you measure the response.

Whether it is adverts, direct mail, Google ads, email marketing, networking or one of the hundreds of alternative channels to market, know which campaign your prospects have responded to, as in most cases the results are repeatable and scalable and you want to get the most '*bang for your buck*'.

☐ **Benefits versus Features** - people respond to the benefits that can be gained from buying a product or service and the pain or problem it fixes not a list of features.

Someone who buys a Porsche or Ferrari is probably interested in the speed (benefit) not the specifications of the engine (feature). Review your marketing material and establish if you are focusing on features rather than the benefits - list every time that you promote a feature and convert it to a benefit, then adapt your marketing messages accordingly.

☐ **References/Testimonials** - people buy from people they trust. To help build confidence, testimonials and references from satisfied customers will enhance your reputation in the market place for a new, potential customer. Use them throughout your marketing, if possible accompanied by a photograph or better still a video of an existing client.

☐ **Case Studies** - to back up any references/testimonials you have, generate some actual case studies of how you have helped your clients. A simple format would be: what was the problem/issue, how did you resolve it, what was the outcome and benefit to the client.

☐ **Guarantee** - reduce the risk of doing business with you by offering a guarantee pertinent to the industry you are in - this is particularly powerful to distinguish you from the competition and could be a number of things: money back, try before you buy, something for free or something else pertinent to your business that has a perceived high value, but which does not cost you as a business to give as a guarantee.

☐ **Referral Strategy** - the strongest from of lead generation that convert to sales are referrals from existing clients, peers, network contacts, partners or anyone that knows your business and is confident in recommending you. If a prospect receives a referral to use you from someone they trust, you have already 'inherited' some of that trust in your ability to supply.

It is possible to put a strategy together that generates referrals in this way and provides a constant supply of leads. Consider where you could generate referrals for your business - when was the last time you asked your current customer base if they could recommend you to anyone in their business network?

☐ **Competition** - be aware of what your competitors are doing in the market place, how you can stay ahead of them and how you would distinguish yourself from them? If you were side by side on the High Street, or if your websites were compared, what would make you stand out and why would someone buy from you rather than your competitor?

☐ **Prospects** - maintain communication with potential customers, only a few prospects will buy as a result of an initial, first time contact. In fact, some interesting statistics are as follows in terms of the percentage of sales that are made versus the number of contacts made with a prospect:

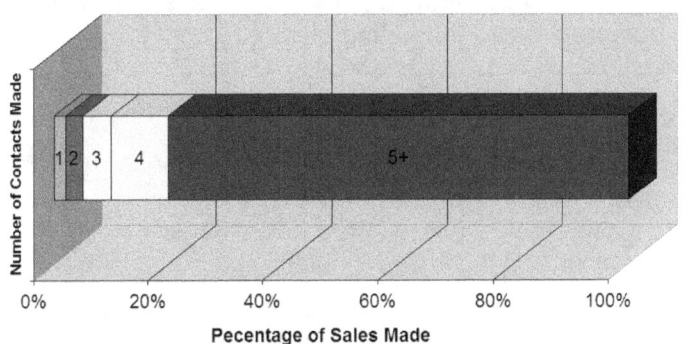

No. of Contacts Made:	1	2	3	4	5+
% of Sales Made:	2%	3%	5%	10%	80%

It has also been reported that people will back down by the third 'no' (if not before) from a potential customer, therefore, if your business is tenacious and sticks with maintaining contact, you can hopefully see the competitive advantage you will glean from your persistence.

To help you with your marketing planning, Marketing Plan Pro is award winning software to assist you in writing a comprehensive marketing plan: http://tinyurl.com/mplanpro

Operations

☐ **Business Systems** - have you got the necessary IT systems to support your business, in particular a back up process that does not rely on a CD that your secretary takes home at weekends?

Only 35% of SMEs have a disaster recovery plan and, if the worse happens, and your vital business data is lost, there is a less than 10% chance that your company will survive! Downtime in any business can lead to loss of orders. Once again, solutions need not be expensive and there are more and more IT companies providing remote IT management to ensure your systems and software are functioning properly and consistently.

☐ **Business Processes** - every business has processes and systems in place across all departments. However, often the way that processes work within a department only exists in the head of certain employees and therefore would pose a problem for the business if they were to move from the job.

Documentation of your business processes need not be cumbersome and once captured becomes less reliant on key individuals and can be compiled to form a useful training manual for future employees and make it easier to have multi-skilled staff to perform essential business functions in the absence of the company 'expert'.

☐ **Supply Chain Management** - any stock in a business is tying up cash - the longer products sit on a shelf, either as raw materials or finished goods, whilst considered an asset, is revenue and profit not earned.

Look at how to make your supply chain (see diagram below) more efficient by managing the logistics more effectively with consignment stock, just in time delivery or kanban systems for example - put the onus on the supplier to take more of the risk and improve your cashflow.

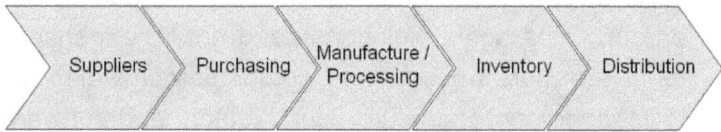

| Suppliers | Purchasing | Manufacture / Processing | Inventory | Distribution |

☐ **Reduce Waste** - this is not just referring to being environmentally friendly and reusing or recycling supplies and consumables where possible, but looking at your business and removing redundant or duplicated business processes.

An example of this is numerous, distributed databases with the same information that are all updated individually and manually - thereby leading to more errors and more than likely having inconsistent data between systems. Time is money and ultimately any time that is wasted is costing your business.

☐ **Answering Service** - often the first impression a prospect gets of your company is when they call you. Who answers the phone in your business, how long does it take to pick the call up, is what is said consistent and does it portray the professional image you are looking to achieve, does the call ever end up going to an answer machine because everyone is too busy to answer it?

When someone is calling they want to speak to a person at the other end and get their problem dealt with - not all businesses have a receptionist or a system of managing incoming calls, therefore it is worth considering an outsourced answering service.

Some interesting statistics:

- o When a call is answered by an automated answering system, 1/3rd of business callers would hang up without leaving message.
- o When a call is not answered at all in the first attempt, 2/3rds of business callers would call a competitor.

This can be a relatively inexpensive solution to managing your calls, with messages being taken in a professional manner and in the name of your company, with the messages being passed on by transferring the call, email or text and a log kept of all calls received, as well as vetting marketing and sales calls. A reasonably priced and cost effective service is http://tinyurl/alldaypa.

Resources

☐ **Recruitment** - hiring the right person first time is not the easiest of jobs, is very time consuming and therefore costly; especially if you make the wrong choice. Job agencies can help with this process but at a cost.

One thing to consider, albeit potentially more expensive, is outsourcing. If this is a possibility for a given role in your business, the benefits it brings can offset any additional costs you may incur i.e. flexibility to increase/decrease the resource. The person(s) in question are suppliers to you not 'dependents', you can choose competitively in the marketplace for the best service for your business and there are no obligations that exist when employing staff.

☐ **HR Legislation** - as tribunals are becoming more common place and the average amount paid out to disgruntled ex-employees continues to rise, having your 'ducks in a row' in relation to current employee legislation may not seem a critical aspect for your business, but it is a legal requirement and could be a wise investment.

The basics - an employee handbook covering policy and procedures, a job description and a contract of employment - can be straightforwardly implemented by an outsourced HR professional.

For a comprehensive service for all your HR needs, please take a look at www.abacus-hr.co.uk.

☐ **Redundancy** - as the word implies, is there 'redundancy' in your business - roles that are no longer required or that are not being fulfilled in an effective way? This can be typical in family run business when friends and family may be employed for emotional and personal reasons rather than business reasons. If you know such a situation is impacting the profitability of your business then appropriate action needs to be taken.

☐ **Staff** - without personnel your business would more than likely not survive and staff are a potentially expensive resource if they are not performing in your business.

Motivation is a key factor and is not necessarily that onerous to achieve. Communicate with your team on a regular basis, letting them know what is happening with the business, even if the news is not so great - they probably already know anyway. Appraise staff and set them targets in line with your business plan and what you want to achieve in each department and reward them accordingly for the contribution that they make - maybe share options are a possibility within your business?

Train and develop staff in line with the business needs. Consider your staff as an investment as opposed to a cost and nurture them so that you get the best return - on the whole people want to do their best at work but sometimes need encouragement. Listen to your staff - particularly with regard to problems that your business is facing - as they are working in the various areas where the problems exist, they are best placed to suggest a solution - you may be surprised how your business could be enhanced.

☐ **Legal** - such services are usually a distress purchase as and when the need arises, however, 'panic buying' doesn't necessarily support finding the best service for your needs. It may be worthwhile spending some time to identify a solicitor or lawyer that can be on hand to work with you as and when required.

Fundamental legal helplines are provided by many trade organisations and membership organisations as part of the yearly subscription e.g. FSB, local Chambers of Commerce, and is worth considering for simple legal matters that may arise so you know your rights for a given situation.

A site to consider for commonly used legal documents that can be customised to your requirement and vetted by a legal expert before release is www.lawsense.co.uk

☐ **Health & Safety** - should you fall foul of the legislation relating to health and safety at work, the 'buck' stops with the business owner, with the most serious breaches that have endangered a person at work can lead to a prison sentence. Whilst this is extreme and rare, having your business assessed in respect of this legal requirement provides you and your staff with peace of mind in the workplace.

A useful article on the basic requirements relating to health and safety can be found here: http://tinyurl.com/health-and-safety-basics.

☐ **Contracts** - the simplest form of contract is your terms & conditions. Are these up to date and do they actually reflect your business and the way you want to interact with your client? Most importantly, is your client base aware of them as this defines payment terms, warranties, etc., that they are effectively 'signing up' to?

In addition, if you are entering into a formal contract with a supplier or customer, have you ensured that it is 'reasonable', fit for purpose and adequately reflects how you want to engage in a business transaction. Such documents are often overlooked but should be considered as negotiable and 'fair' to all parties concerned as well as providing a level of protection should a deal not go as planned.

Even though contracts are considered legally binding, they do not necessarily need expensive lawyers to get involved to vet and negotiate on your behalf, there are specialists in contractual arrangements that can provide lower cost and legitimate advice than a fully fledged lawyer; for example www.devant.co.uk.

Personal

☐ **Time Management** - the only thing you don't have more of in a day is time! How you use this time is down to you. Chances are, given the amount of hours you work and the amount of money you take out of the business, you are one of the lowest paid staff as an hourly rate! Focus your time in line with what your objectives are for the business as the owner of the company - don't spend your time fire fighting and trying to keep all the 'plates spinning'.

Working 'on' the business as opposed to 'in' it, will benefit you in the long run - allowing you to take a 'helicopter' view of the business and where you want it to be strategically. The most powerful tools you have to achieve this are the ability to say "'No" and the art of delegation.

☐ **Training & Development** - you are never too old to learn and you don't know all there is to know about running a business and being a leader. Look at the areas where you could develop your skills - time management, communication, stress management, leadership and so on?

Having someone to bounce ideas off of, share business issues and problems with and generally be an 'ear to bend' or 'shoulder to cry on' can be of real benefit and let you know that you are not on your own feeling lonely and frustrated at the top – therefore, consider setting up a peer network or advisory board or, failing that maybe a coach, mentor or business advisor to support you with your business aspirations.

☐ **Be Innovative** - there are many tools that help facilitate innovation. These can be used to improve the performance of your business and help you stay ahead of the competition.

The most commonly used tool is brainstorming, which should involve as many people as feasible, including staff from different areas on the business. All ideas should be allowed to be put forward in the first instance without judgment, before refining, prioritising and adopting. A useful site for other tools is www.innovationtools.com.

☐ **Work/Life Balance** - a bit of a cliché but still relevant in today's business world. Manage where you spend your time and don't lose out on your family, friends and your life. 'Work to live' not vice versa. If you are healthy and not so stressed, this will be reflected in your business and support your path to independence, wealth and achieving your vision.

Bonus Tip

☐ **Have fun!** - there is no law in business that says you can't enjoy what you're doing and be successful at the same time!

Summary

Hopefully you have found this guide beneficial and it has inspired you to take action and change you and your business today.

There is no point in finding these tips intellectually stimulating but not putting anything into action that could make a difference to your business.

You have a choice: do nothing or do something? Unfortunately, experience tells me that most business owners surprisingly do nothing and continue with things as they are. With regard to the latter point, you can do this on your own or get some help with the implementation of some of the points that have been covered.

It is not feasible to make everything happen in one go, it is easier if broken down in to 'bite size' chunks and approached systematically (remembering that delegation is a powerful tool!).

Therefore from the advice that has been covered in this guide, prioritise those tips that you believe will make the most impact to the performance of your business - establish what are the 'now' actions and what are the 'next' actions, then decide who is going to take the action, by when the action will be completed and how you can measure that a difference is being made and finally, document it.

You should now be in possession of a one page business plan! This is a 'dynamic' document that you can use as a step by step action plan to make things happen in your business and regularly review the progress and update accordingly.

It may be something to share with staff as an incentive for you, as the person overall accountable, to get the job done and to encourage staff by showing that changes are happening that will benefit the business and ultimately them.

Good luck with the success of your business.

Paul

About The Author

 Paul Green is an experienced business expert and is the founder partner of UK Business Advisors (UKBA™), Fellow of the Institute for Independent Business (IIB) and a Personal Business Advisor for the Effective Business Group.

He has personally worked with over 40 business owners and can improve your <u>profitability within 60 days</u>........or your <u>money back</u>!

With a pedigree earned over 20 years within the electronics industry, Paul has worked with many corporate organisations as a consultant. He now spends most of his time in the SME sector, typically working with MDs and Owners of companies with more than 5 staff or a turnover in excess of £250k. His specialisation is in strategic and business planning, sales assessment and performance, mentoring/coaching and leadership development. Whilst he is based in the East Midlands, he has access to an extensive network of business professionals across the UK (and worldwide) that can offer business support across all 'pillars' of a business: strategy, finance, sales, marketing, operations, resources and management.

Recently he has become a columnist for 'We Know Business' magazine - www.weknowbusiness.co.uk and Effective Business Today - www.effectivebusinesstoday.com.

Contact Details

If you are looking for hands on, practical and action based business advice please make contact today for an **initial free and no obligation meeting** with an independent business expert to discuss your business.

t: 0333 444 8522

m: 07949 703137

e: me@paulgreen.co.uk

w: www.paulgreen.biz

skype: pgreen1964

LinkedIn: www.linkedin.com/in/pgreen1964

Twitter: twitter.com/paulgreen

Facebook: www.facebook.com/paul.green.uk

40

References

Here are some sample testimonials from a few of the clients worked with over the years:

"Working with the management team, Paul has been able to add value to our organisation by providing a broad overview and being a listening ear to our issues. I would have no hesitation recommending him to other businesses".

Trevor Proudfoot, MD - Cliveden Conservation
www.clivedenconservation.co.uk

"With his sales experience and coaching skills, Paul has supported us in implementing a successful sales pipeline management system from lead generation through to customer order".

Mark Hall, Sales Director - Embassy Freight
www.embassyfreight.co.uk

"Working with the Paul allowed us to improve our time management and day to day systems and processes. Having someone to bounce ideas off and access to an independent set of eyes looking in, enabled us to develop our business and look towards the future. He has contributed to the way in which we communicate with the staff team and advised us on various managerial challenges. Currently we are working with him on a marketing plan for our organisation".

Rob & Joanna Brown, Proprietors - Marlow Day Nursery
www.marlowdaynursery.co.uk

Success Stories

Please find below a selection of case studies from actual clients:

Strategic Planning – Telecom Industry

Worked directly with the managing director of a company specialising in Software as a Service (SaaS) to the telecoms industry. Facilitated a strategic plan for the business to help raise funding, identify growth areas, improve financial reporting and focus the sales effort.

The plan was successfully presented to the bank enabling a loan to be offered. The company increased their sales by 20% in the first year.

Sales Performance Improvement – Freight Forwarding

The sales director needed support in managing the pipeline for the business. Most of the sales relied on his direct input and recruitment of sales people had not been successful.

The existing customer base was analysed to identify upselling opportunities, new target prospects were identified and a sales plan generated, a CRM system was implemented and a pipeline management system was put in place.

Sales increased by 15% in the first year and 40% in the second, with profits doubling in that period of time.

Operational Improvement – Conservation Company

The managing director was frustrated with the performance of his staff both back office and out in the field. A review of the whole business was undertaken to identify key business processes, duplication of effort and areas for administrative and communication improvement. This was documented allowing for specific roles and business requirements to be identified.

This resulted in a restructuring of the staff roles and a significant improvement in the way departments interacted with each other. The changes were communicated with staff leading to an improved morale amongst the team. Efficiencies made improved the profitability of the business.

Acknowledgements

Thanks go to my many business colleagues and associates from UKBA™, the IIB and LinkedIn who have help with the content and compilation of this guide.

Useful Resources

Boost Your Business Blog: www.paulgreen.biz/blog

Article Directory: www.paulgreen.biz/articles

Free Downloads: www.paulgreen.biz/downloads.htm

Useful Links

UK Business Advisors – UKBA™ is a group of over 80 independent business advisors throughout the UK who have been selected based on their track record, experience and the range of skills they provide covering all aspects of business – finance, sales, marketing, operations, resources, strategy and management.

www.ukba.co.uk

Institute for Independent Business – the IIB is a not-for-profit research, training and accreditation organisation. Thousands of experienced executives from every type of business discipline have been trained by the Institute, they have graduated from an IIB Residential Business School to advise and help small to medium sized businesses.

www.iib.org.ws

Effective Business Group – EBG is a unique group of over 100,000 Managing Directors of SMEs who want to 'Grow Their Business'. The network is a dynamic, connected community of businesses focused on promotion, communication, and growth. The intention is to increase the revenue, profit, and value of the members' businesses.

www.effectivebusinessgroup.com

Free Business Review

If you are a managing director or business owner of a company with over 5 staff and/or a turnover in excess of £250k you are entitled to a free business review with an experienced, independent business expert.

This will take up no more than a couple of hours of your time and will be an opportunity to discuss all aspects of your business (in confidence) with a business advisor who has experience of running their own business, so they know what it feels like to be at the head of a company when the 'buck' ultimately stops with you.

Your time is valuable and therefore the intention is to learn about your business, understand the problems you may be facing and to offer some guidance to you (if possible) on the day. It is unlikely that they will have an on the spot solution, however, whatever it is that's keeping you awake at night, if the person who conducts the review with you cannot directly help, they have access to an extensive network of business professionals covering all industry sectors, specialist disciplines and geographic regions (worldwide if needed).

To book your free, no obligation meeting – please do one of the following:

Call **0333 444 8522** and ask for **Paul Green**

Email review@paulgreen.biz

Go online to: www.paulgreen.biz/review.htm

www.ingramcontent.com/pod-product-compliance
Lightning Source LLC
Chambersburg PA
CBHW051252170526
45165CB00004B/1674